DATE: ___ / ___ / ___

Asshole of the Day

(name of person)

Today's Clusterfuck

_____

_____

_____

_____

_____

MY CURRENT MOOD

1 🖕 🖕 🖕 🖕 🖕 🖕 🖕 🖕 🖕 🖕 10

Shit List
people and things

1. _____

2. _____

3. _____

4. _____

5. _____

Word of the Day
Check all that apply...

☐ SHITTY   ☐ DOUCHEBAG

BRAINFART ☐   BITCHNUGGET ☐

☐ DAMNIT   ☐ FUCKED

ASSHOLE ☐   SHITSTORM ☐

☐ CLUSTERFUCK   ☐ _____

Bright Spots... It wasn't all bad, was it?

_____
_____
_____
_____
_____
_____
_____
_____
_____

Shit to Do

☐ _____
☐ _____
☐ _____
☐ _____
☐ _____
☐ _____

I'm fortunate to have:

Get your mind off shit & unscramble profanity:

EUFCKAFC

answer: fuckface

A
GrATTITUDE
Journal
to
help
you
fight
back
against
all
the
madness.

Take
back
your
day
with
this
daily,
guided,
fill-in
journal!

Gratitude
w/
attitude

DATE: ___ / ___ / ___

DAY OF THE WEEK
S M T W TH F S

AM
PM

Idiot of the Moment

(name of person)

Today's Shitty Situation

_____
_____
_____
_____
_____

MY CURRENT MOOD

1 🖕 🖕 🖕 🖕 🖕 🖕 🖕 🖕 🖕 🖕 10

Shit List
people and things

1. _____
2. _____
3. _____
4. _____
5. _____

>>>>>BRAIN FART OF THE DAY<<<<<

Bright Spots... It wasn't all bad, was it?

_____

_____

_____

_____

_____

_____

_____

_____

> "You got to pay me double and provide a stink suit to haul your shit."

I'm fortunate to have:

Get your mind off shit w/ some this and that: _Saturdays or Sundays? Stuff animals or dolls? Chocolate or vanilla? Fish or birds? Thunderstorms or sunshine? White bread or wheat bread? Walk a dog or rock a baby? Theme park or water park? Rain or shine?_

DATE: ___/___/___

First Fucktart I thought of today...

(name of person)

Today's Fucking Debacle

_____
_____
_____
_____
_____

MY CURRENT MOOD

1 ✋ ✋ ✋ ✋ ✋ ✋ ✋ ✋ ✋ ✋ 10

Shit List
people and things

1. _____
2. _____
3. _____
4. _____
5. _____

Crap that Happened
Check all that apply...

☐ TREATED UNFAIRLY ☐ PAID BILL

GOT A TICKET ☐ SUCKERPUNCHED ☐

☐ ACCIDENT BACKSTABBED ☐

PUNISHED ☐ LATE FOR WORK ☐

☐ LOST A BET ☐ _____

Bright Spots... It wasn't all bad, was it?

_____
_____
_____
_____
_____
_____
_____
_____
_____

Shit to Do

I'm fortunate to have:

- ☐ _____
- ☐ _____
- ☐ _____
- ☐ _____
- ☐ _____
- ☐ _____

Get your mind off shit & unscramble profanity:

TIUHLLSB

DATE: ___/___/___

DAY OF THE WEEK

S M T W TH F S

AM
PM

Jackass of the Week

(name of person)

Today's ___ Fiasco

_____
_____
_____
_____
_____

MY CURRENT MOOD

1  10

Shit List
people and things

1. _____
2. _____
3. _____
4. _____
5. _____

"
_____
_____
"

VERBAL DIARRHEA of the DAY

Bright Spots... It wasn't all bad, was it?

_____

_____

_____

_____

_____

_____

_____

_____

> " Some days I have no fucking clue what I'm doing. And other days, I'm completely dumbfounded. "

I'm fortunate to have:

Get your mind off shit w/ some this and that: Laundry or dishes? Car or truck? Air dry or hair dryer? Video games or computer games? Witches or wizards? Pandas or whales? Reading or writing? Alaska or Hawaii? Matches or lighters? Fishing or hunting? Guitar or violin?

Bright Spots... It wasn't all bad, was it?

_____

_____

_____

_____

_____

_____

_____

_____

_____

Shit to Do

I'm fortunate to have:

- ☐ _____
- ☐ _____
- ☐ _____
- ☐ _____
- ☐ _____
- ☐ _____

Get your mind off shit & unscramble profanity:

SSEALOH

answer: asshole

DATE: ___ / ___ / ___

DAY OF THE WEEK
S M T W TH F S

AM
PM

Dipshit of the Day

_____
(name of person)

Today's Clusterfuck

_____
_____
_____
_____
_____

MY CURRENT MOOD

1 🖕 🖕 🖕 🖕 🖕 🖕 🖕 🖕 🖕 🖕 10

Shit List
people and things

1. _____
2. _____
3. _____
4. _____
5. _____

Word of the Day
Check all that apply...

☐ SHITTY   ☐ DOUCHEBAG
BRAINFART ☐   BITCHNUGGET ☐
☐ DAMNIT   ☐ FUCKED
ASSHOLE ☐   SHITSTORM ☐
☐ CLUSTERFUCK   ☐ _____

Bright Spots... It wasn't all bad, was it?

_____

_____

_____

_____

_____

_____

_____

_____

> ## If there was money to be made as a 'swearing sailor,' I'd be retired by now!

I'm fortunate to have:

Get your mind off shit w/ some this and that: Drinking or eating? Roller skating or ice skating? Forest or jungle? Meat or fish? Salt or pepper? Staples or paper clips? Nice car or house? Romance or action? Puzzles or board games? Soy milk or almond milk?

DATE: _____ / _____ / _____

DAY OF THE WEEK

S M T W TH F S

AM
PM

Shitbreath who got too close...

(name of person)

Today's Shitty Situation

_____
_____
_____
_____
_____

MY CURRENT MOOD

1 🖕 🖕 🖕 🖕 🖕 🖕 🖕 🖕 🖕 🖕 10

Shit List
people and things

1. _____
2. _____
3. _____
4. _____
5. _____

>>>>>BRAIN FART OF THE DAY<<<<<

Bright Spots... It wasn't all bad, was it?

_____
_____
_____
_____
_____
_____
_____
_____
_____

Shit to Do

I'm fortunate to have:

- ☐ _____
- ☐ _____
- ☐ _____
- ☐ _____
- ☐ _____
- ☐ _____

Get your mind off shit & unscramble profanity:

CHDDIKAE

answer: dickhead

DATE: ___ / ___ / ___

DAY OF THE WEEK

S M T W TH F S

AM
PM

Twatlip of the Hour

(name of person)

Today's Fucking Debacle

_____

_____

_____

_____

_____

MY CURRENT MOOD

1   10

Shit List
people and things

1. _____

2. _____

3. _____

4. _____

5. _____

Crap that Happened
Check all that apply...

☐ TREATED UNFAIRLY   ☐ PAID BILL

GOT A TICKET ☐   SUCKERPUNCHED ☐

☐ ACCIDENT   ☐ BACKSTABBED

PUNISHED ☐   LATE FOR WORK ☐

☐ LOST A BET   ☐ _____

_____

_____

_____

_____

_____

_____

_____

_____

> ❝ I'm at a whole new level of "I don't give a fuck. ❞

I'm fortunate to have:

Get your mind off shit w/ some this and that: Lamps or candles? Truth or lie? Summer or winter? No food or no sleep? Checks or stripes? Sleep or play? Serious or funny? Air conditioner or ceiling fan? Necklace or bracelets? Rice or noodles? White or brown rice?

DATE: ___ / ___ / ___

DAY OF THE WEEK

S M T W TH F S

AM

PM

Dipshit of the Moment

(name of person)

Today's [ ] Fiasco

_____
_____
_____
_____
_____

MY CURRENT MOOD

1 ✊ ✊ ✊ ✊ ✊ ✊ ✊ ✊ ✊ ✊ 10

Shit List
people and things

1. _____
2. _____
3. _____
4. _____
5. _____

"

"

VERBAL DIARRHEA of the DAY

Bright Spots... It wasn't all bad, was it?

_____
_____
_____
_____
_____
_____
_____
_____
_____

Shit to Do

I'm fortunate to have:

- [ ] _____
- [ ] _____
- [ ] _____
- [ ] _____
- [ ] _____
- [ ] _____

Get your mind off shit &
unscramble profanity:

TIHCB

answer: bitch

DATE: _____ / _____ / _____

DAY OF THE WEEK
S M T W TH F S

AM
PM

_____ of the Moment

(name of person)

Today's Crappy Moment

_____

_____

_____

_____

_____

MY CURRENT MOOD

1  10

Shit List
people and things

1. _____

2. _____

3. _____

4. _____

5. _____

Phrase of the Day
Check one...

☐ WHAT THE FUCK   ☐ YOU SUCK ASS

FUCK OFF ☐   WTF R U DOING? ☐

☐ WHO GIVES A SHIT   ☐ EAT SHIT

NICE TRY, DICK ☐   GET THE FUCK OUT ☐

☐ _____

Bright Spots... It wasn't all bad, was it?

_____

_____

_____

_____

_____

_____

_____

_____

"This is an asshole free zone. Bye bye!"

I'm fortunate to have:

Get your mind off shit w/ some this and that: Cookies or ice cream? Lost or found? Giving or receiving? Spring or summer? Party person or small gatherings? Library or museum? Wealth or happiness? Skates or bike? Blanket or comforter? Introvert or extrovert?

Bright Spots... It wasn't all bad, was it?

_____
_____
_____
_____
_____
_____
_____
_____
_____

Shit to Do

- [ ] _____
- [ ] _____
- [ ] _____
- [ ] _____
- [ ] _____
- [ ] _____

I'm fortunate to have:

Get your mind off shit & unscramble profanity:

IHASEHTD

answer: shithead

DATE: ___ / ___ / ___

DAY OF THE WEEK

S M T W TH F S

AM
PM

Fuckface of the Week

(name of person)

Today's Shitty Situation

_____

_____

_____

_____

_____

MY CURRENT MOOD

1  10

Shit List
people and things

1. _____

2. _____

3. _____

4. _____

5. _____

>>>>>BRAIN FART OF THE DAY<<<<<

Bright Spots... It wasn't all bad, was it?

_____

_____

_____

_____

_____

_____

_____

_____

" My biggest accomplish-ment was a clusterfuck. "

I'm fortunate to have:

Get your mind off shit w/ some this and that: Formal or casual? Musician or actor? Motel or hotel? Hot cocoa or coffee? Snowball or water balloon? Ninja or samurai? Snowboarding or surfing? Sit-ups or push ups? Cold or flu? New York or London? Logical or creative?

Bright Spots... It wasn't all bad, was it?

_____
_____
_____
_____
_____
_____
_____
_____
_____

Shit to Do

I'm fortunate to have:

- [ ] _____
- [ ] _____
- [ ] _____
- [ ] _____
- [ ] _____
- [ ] _____

Get your mind off shit &
unscramble profanity:

AEPSSWI

answer: asswipe

DATE: ___ / ___ / ___

DAY OF THE WEEK
S M T W TH F S

○ AM PM

Fucktart of the Moment

(name of person)

Today's [ ] Fiasco

_____
_____
_____
_____
_____

MY CURRENT MOOD

1  10

Shit List
people and things

1. _____

2. _____

3. _____

4. _____

5. _____

"

"

VERBAL DIARRHEA OF THE DAY

Bright Spots... It wasn't all bad, was it?

_____

_____

_____

_____

_____

_____

_____

_____

" **Fuck this shit and fuck it sideways.** "

I'm fortunate to have:

Get your mind off shit w/ some this and that: *Home cooked or takeout? Glasses or contacts? Kitten or puppy? Detailed or abstract? Sunglasses or sun visor? Ice cream or popsicle? Selfies or group photos? Early bird or night owl? Adventurous or cautious? Pencil or pen?*

DATE: ___/___/___

DAY OF THE WEEK

S M T W TH F S

○ AM
PM

Bullshit Award

(name of person)

Today's Crappy Moment

_____

_____

_____

_____

_____

MY CURRENT MOOD

1 🖕 🖕 🖕 🖕 🖕 🖕 🖕 🖕 🖕 🖕 10

Shit List
people and things

1. _____

2. _____

3. _____

4. _____

5. _____

Phrase of the Day
Check one...

☐ WHAT THE FUCK   ☐ YOU SUCK ASS

FUCK OFF ☐   WTF R U DOING? ☐

☐ WHO GIVES A SHIT   ☐ EAT SHIT

NICE TRY, DICK ☐   GET THE FUCK OUT ☐

☐ _____

Bright Spots... It wasn't all bad, was it?

_____

_____

_____

_____

_____

_____

_____

_____

_____

Shit to Do

I'm fortunate to have:

- [ ] _____
- [ ] _____
- [ ] _____
- [ ] _____
- [ ] _____
- [ ] _____

Get your mind off shit & unscramble profanity:

KTELCCFRSUU

answer: clusterfuck

DATE: ___/___/___

DAY OF THE WEEK
S M T W TH F S

AM
PM

Dickweed of the Day

(name of person)

Today's Clusterfuck

_____
_____
_____
_____

MY CURRENT MOOD

1 🖕 🖕 🖕 🖕 🖕 🖕 🖕 🖕 🖕 🖕 10

Shit List
people and things

1. _____
2. _____
3. _____
4. _____
5. _____

Word of the Day
Check all that apply...

☐ SHITTY   ☐ DOUCHEBAG
  BRAINFART ☐   BITCHNUGGET ☐
☐ DAMNIT   ☐ FUCKED
  ASSHOLE ☐   SHITSTORM ☐
☐ CLUSTERFUCK   ☐ _____

Bright Spots... It wasn't all bad, was it?

_____

_____

_____

_____

_____

_____

_____

_____

"Hey fucker, do you miss me yet?"

I'm fortunate to have:

Get your mind off shit w/ some this and that: Camping or hiking? Wedding or birthday? Sneakers or boots? Silver or gold? Kids or pets? Fly or teleportation? Tent or RV? Pink or blue? Sweet or sour? Comedy or chic flick? Cupcake or Muffin? Fast or slow? Rock or hip hop?

DATE: ____ / ____ / ____

DAY OF THE WEEK

S M T W TH F S

○ AM PM

First Asshole I thought of today...

(name of person)

Today's Shitty Situation

_____

_____

_____

_____

_____

MY CURRENT MOOD

1 🖕 🖕 🖕 🖕 🖕 🖕 🖕 🖕 🖕 🖕 10

Shit List
people and things

1. _____

2. _____

3. _____

4. _____

5. _____

>>>>>BRAIN FART OF THE DAY<<<<<

Bright Spots... It wasn't all bad, was it?

_____
_____
_____
_____
_____
_____
_____
_____
_____

Shit to Do

I'm fortunate to have:

- [ ] _____
- [ ] _____
- [ ] _____
- [ ] _____
- [ ] _____
- [ ] _____

Get your mind off shit & unscramble profanity:

LSCASWON

DATE: ___ / ___ / ___

DAY OF THE WEEK
S M T W TH F S

AM
PM

Idiot of the Moment

(name of person)

Today's Fucking Debacle

_____
_____
_____
_____
_____

MY CURRENT MOOD

1  10

Shit List
people and things

1. _____
2. _____
3. _____
4. _____
5. _____

Crap that Happened
Check all that apply...

☐ TREATED UNFAIRLY ☐ PAID BILL

GOT A TICKET ☐ SUCKERPUNCHED ☐

☐ ACCIDENT ☐ BACKSTABBED

PUNISHED ☐ LATE FOR WORK ☐

☐ LOST A BET ☐ _____

Bright Spots... It wasn't all bad, was it?

_____

_____

_____

_____

_____

_____

_____

_____

"You're looking for trouble? Where can I sign up?"

I'm fortunate to have:

Get your mind off shit w/ some this and that: _Online or in store shopping? Dress or pants? Chair or coach? Chips or trail mix? Cardio or strength? Hammer or nail? Gummy worms or gummy bears? Vacation or stay at home? Crossword or word search? Sculpture or painting?_

DATE: ____ / ____ / ____

DAY OF THE WEEK
S M T W TH F S

AM
PM

_____ of the Day

(name of person)

Today's [ ] Fiasco

_____
_____
_____
_____
_____

MY CURRENT MOOD

1 👆 👆 👆 👆 👆 👆 👆 👆 👆 👆 10

Shit List
people and things

1. _____
2. _____
3. _____
4. _____
5. _____

"

"

VERBAL DIARRHEA of the DAY

_____
_____
_____
_____
_____
_____
_____
_____

Shit to Do

I'm fortunate to have:

- ☐ _____
- ☐ _____
- ☐ _____
- ☐ _____
- ☐ _____
- ☐ _____

Get your mind off shit & unscramble profanity:

UCERFK

answer: fucker

DATE: ___ / ___ / ___

DAY OF THE WEEK

S M T W TH F S

AM
PM

Prick of the Week

(name of person)

Today's Crappy Moment

_____
_____
_____
_____
_____

MY CURRENT MOOD

1 🖕 🖕 🖕 🖕 🖕 🖕 🖕 🖕 🖕 🖕 10

Shit List
people and things

1. _____
2. _____
3. _____
4. _____
5. _____

Phrase of the Day
Check one...

☐ WHAT THE FUCK ☐ YOU SUCK ASS

FUCK OFF ☐ WTF R U DOING? ☐

☐ WHO GIVES A SHIT ☐ EAT SHIT

NICE TRY, DICK ☐ GET THE FUCK OUT ☐

☐ _____

Bright Spots... It wasn't all bad, was it?

_____
_____
_____
_____
_____
_____
_____
_____

> "Kick the shit out of fear and celebrate with a margarita."

I'm fortunate to have:

Get your mind off shit w/ some this and that: Bottle or glass? Moose or hedgehog? French bread or Sourdough? Hash browns or French Fries? Live or recorded? Dressed up or dressed down? Coffee or tea? Baked or fried? Solar system or Galaxy? Mosquitos or bees?

DATE: ___ / ___ / ___

DAY OF THE WEEK

S M T W TH F S

AM
PM

Asshole of the Hour

(name of person)

Today's Clusterfuck

_____
_____
_____
_____
_____

MY CURRENT MOOD

1 10

Shit List
people and things

1. _____
2. _____
3. _____
4. _____
5. _____

Word of the Day
Check all that apply...

☐ SHITTY   ☐ DOUCHEBAG
BRAINFART ☐   BITCHNUGGET ☐
☐ DAMNIT   ☐ FUCKED
ASSHOLE ☐   SHITSTORM ☐
☐ CLUSTERFUCK   ☐ _____

Bright Spots... It wasn't all bad, was it?

_____
_____
_____
_____
_____
_____
_____
_____
_____

Shit to Do

I'm fortunate to have:

- ☐ _____
- ☐ _____
- ☐ _____
- ☐ _____
- ☐ _____
- ☐ _____

Get your mind off shit & unscramble profanity:

PTTAILW

answer: twatlip

DATE: ___ / ___ / ___

DAY OF THE WEEK

S M T W TH F S

AM
PM

Shitbrain of the Day

(name of person)

Today's Shitty Situation

_____

_____

_____

_____

_____

MY CURRENT MOOD

1  10

Shit List
people and things

1. _____

2. _____

3. _____

4. _____

5. _____

>>>>>BRAIN FART OF THE DAY<<<<<

Bright Spots... It wasn't all bad, was it?

> ## I know I ain't shit but I got flies all around me.

I'm fortunate to have:

Get your mind off shit w/ some this and that: Rich or superpowers? Peanut butter or jelly? Singing or listening music? Medium rare or well done steak? Old or young? Rent or buy? Guitar or bass? Sweet or savory? Home or hotel? Books or movies? Email or letter? Hairdo or hat?

DATE: ___ / ___ / ___

DAY OF THE WEEK

S M T W TH F S

AM
PM

Bastard Award

(name of person)

Today's Fucking Debacle

_____
_____
_____
_____
_____

MY CURRENT MOOD

1 🖕 🖕 🖕 🖕 🖕 🖕 🖕 🖕 🖕 🖕 10

Shit List
people and things

1. _____
2. _____
3. _____
4. _____
5. _____

Crap that Happened
Check all that apply...

☐ TREATED UNFAIRLY ☐ PAID BILL

GOT A TICKET ☐   SUCKERPUNCHED ☐

☐ ACCIDENT   ☐ BACKSTABBED

PUNISHED ☐   LATE FOR WORK ☐

☐ LOST A BET   ☐ _____

Bright Spots... It wasn't all bad, was it?

_____

_____

_____

_____

_____

_____

_____

_____

Shit to Do

I'm fortunate to have:

☐ _____

☐ _____

☐ _____

☐ _____

☐ _____

☐ _____

Get your mind off shit & unscramble profanity:

CDOUAEGBH

DATE: ___ / ___ / ___

DAY OF THE WEEK
S M T W TH F S

AM
PM

Dickhead of the Moment

(name of person)

Today's [ ] Fiasco

_____
_____
_____
_____
_____

MY CURRENT MOOD

1 2 3 4 5 6 7 8 9 10

Shit List
people and things

1. _____
2. _____
3. _____
4. _____
5. _____

"
                    "

VERBAL DIARRHEA of the DAY

Bright Spots... It wasn't all bad, was it?

_____

_____

_____

_____

_____

_____

_____

_____

> There is no way for you to gauge how much I 'don't give a shit' about you or your problems.

I'm fortunate to have:

Get your mind off shit w/ some this and that: Fridays or Saturdays? Roses or sunflowers? Zombies or robots? Protein or carb? Shark or whale? Single or relationship? Sugar or spice? Organize or messy? Body wash or soap? Credit card or cash? Toothpaste or deodorant?

DATE: ___ / ___ / ___

DAY OF THE WEEK

S M T W TH F S

AM

PM

Bitch of the Hour

(name of person)

Today's Crappy Moment

_____

_____

_____

_____

_____

MY CURRENT MOOD

1  10

Shit List
people and things

1. _____

2. _____

3. _____

4. _____

5. _____

Phrase of the Day
Check one...

☐ WHAT THE FUCK   ☐ YOU SUCK ASS

FUCK OFF ☐   WTF R U DOING? ☐

☐ WHO GIVES A SHIT   ☐ EAT SHIT

NICE TRY, DICK ☐   GET THE FUCK OUT ☐

☐ _____

Bright Spots... It wasn't all bad, was it?

_____
_____
_____
_____
_____
_____
_____
_____

Shit to Do

I'm fortunate to have:

- [ ] _____
- [ ] _____
- [ ] _____
- [ ] _____
- [ ] _____
- [ ] _____

Get your mind off shit & unscramble profanity:

ASTAHS

answer: asshat

DATE: _____ / ___ / ___

First Douchebag I thought of Today...

(name of person)

Today's Clusterfuck

_____

_____

_____

_____

MY CURRENT MOOD

1 👆 👆 👆 👆 👆 👆 👆 👆 👆 👆 10

Shit List
people and things

1. _____

2. _____

3. _____

4. _____

5. _____

Word of the Day
Check all that apply...

☐ SHITTY   ☐ DOUCHEBAG

BRAINFART ☐   BITCHNUGGET ☐

☐ DAMNIT   ☐ FUCKED

ASSHOLE ☐   SHITSTORM ☐

☐ CLUSTERFUCK   ☐ _____

Bright Spots... It wasn't all bad, was it?

_____

_____

_____

_____

_____

_____

_____

_____

" I drink straight from the 'I don't give a fuck' bottle. "

I'm fortunate to have:

Get your mind off shit w/ some this and that: Radio or television? Zombies or aliens? Cruise ship or resort? Cute or beautiful? Comedy or horror? Ocean or lake? Comedy or drama? Wallet or purse? Fast food or homemade? BBQ or restaurant? Concert or museum?

DATE: ___ / ___ / ___

DAY OF THE WEEK

S M T W TH F S

AM
PM

Asshole of the Day

(name of person)

Today's Shitty Situation

_____
_____
_____
_____
_____

MY CURRENT MOOD

1  10

Shit List
people and things

1. _____
2. _____
3. _____
4. _____
5. _____

>>>>>BRAIN FART OF THE DAY<<<<<

Bright Spots... It wasn't all bad, was it?

_____
_____
_____
_____
_____
_____
_____
_____
_____

Shit to Do

I'm fortunate to have:

- ☐ _____
- ☐ _____
- ☐ _____
- ☐ _____
- ☐ _____
- ☐ _____

Get your mind off shit & unscramble profanity:

KDWEDICE

answer: dickweed

_____

_____

_____

_____

_____

_____

_____

_____

"What time is it? It's "What the Fuck' O'Clock."

I'm fortunate to have:

Get your mind off shit w/ some this and that: Scrub or wipe? Jupiter or Saturn? Left handed or right handed? Charisma or luck? Dinosaurs or sea monsters? Cloth or paper? Rain or snow? Work hard or play hard? Hard worker or smart worker? Desktop or laptop?

DATE: ____/____/____

Idiot of the Moment

(name of person)

Today's [ ] Fiasco

_____

_____

_____

_____

_____

MY CURRENT MOOD

1 👆 👆 👆 👆 👆 👆 👆 👆 👆 👆 10

Shit List
people and things

1. _____

2. _____

3. _____

4. _____

5. _____

" _____ "

VERBAL DIARRHEA of the DAY

Bright Spots... It wasn't all bad, was it?

_____
_____
_____
_____
_____
_____
_____
_____
_____

Shit to Do

I'm fortunate to have:

- [ ] _____
- [ ] _____
- [ ] _____
- [ ] _____
- [ ] _____
- [ ] _____

Get your mind off shit & unscramble profanity:

ODIIT

answer: idiot

DATE: ____ / ____ / ____

DAY OF THE WEEK
S M T W TH F S

AM
PM

First Snotrag I noticed today...

(name of person)

Today's Crappy Moment

_____

_____

_____

_____

_____

MY CURRENT MOOD

1 🖕 🖕 🖕 🖕 🖕 🖕 🖕 🖕 🖕 🖕 10

Shit List
people and things

1. _____

2. _____

3. _____

4. _____

5. _____

Phrase of the Day
Check one...

☐ WHAT THE FUCK   ☐ YOU SUCK ASS

FUCK OFF ☐   WTF R U DOING? ☐

☐ WHO GIVES A SHIT ☐ EAT SHIT

NICE TRY, DICK ☐   GET THE FUCK OUT ☐

☐ _____

Bright Spots... It wasn't all bad, was it?

_____

_____

_____

_____

_____

_____

_____

" You're like a vibrator. Completely useless unless you're turned on. "

I'm fortunate to have:

Get your mind off shit w/ some this and that: _Cookies or cake? Earthquake or tornado? Flying or turn invisible? Day or night? Purple or green? Laptop or phone? Buttons or snaps? Arcade or movie theatre? Drawing or photography? Riches or Happiness?_

DATE: ___ / ___ / ___

DAY OF THE WEEK

S M T W TH F S

AM
PM

Jackass of the Week

(name of person)

Today's Clusterfuck

_____

_____

_____

_____

_____

MY CURRENT MOOD

1 ☝ ☝ ☝ ☝ ☝ ☝ ☝ ☝ ☝ ☝ 10

Shit List
people and things

1. _____

2. _____

3. _____

4. _____

5. _____

Word of the Day
Check all that apply...

☐ SHITTY   ☐ DOUCHEBAG

BRAINFART ☐   BITCHNUGGET ☐

☐ DAMNIT   ☐ FUCKED

ASSHOLE ☐   SHITSTORM ☐

☐ CLUSTERFUCK   ☐ _____

Bright Spots... It wasn't all bad, was it?

_____
_____
_____
_____
_____
_____
_____
_____
_____

Shit to Do

I'm fortunate to have:

- ☐ _____
- ☐ _____
- ☐ _____
- ☐ _____
- ☐ _____
- ☐ _____

Get your mind off shit & unscramble profanity:

ITSASBHC

answer: bitchass

_____

_____

_____

_____

_____

_____

_____

_____

> "Ha ha ha ha ha ha ha ha ha ha ha ha ha ha, fuck you."

I'm fortunate to have:

Get your mind off shit w/ some this and that: Apples or oranges? Butterflies or caterpillars? Bacon or eggs? Documentary or biography? Sour cream or salsa? Passive or defiant? Ferris wheels or roller coaster? Fire pit or fireplace? Weird or normal? Reality or drama?

DATE: ___ / ___ / ___

DAY OF THE WEEK

S M T W TH F S

AM
PM

Fucktart I Encountered

(name of person)

Today's Fucking Debacle

_____

_____

_____

_____

_____

MY CURRENT MOOD

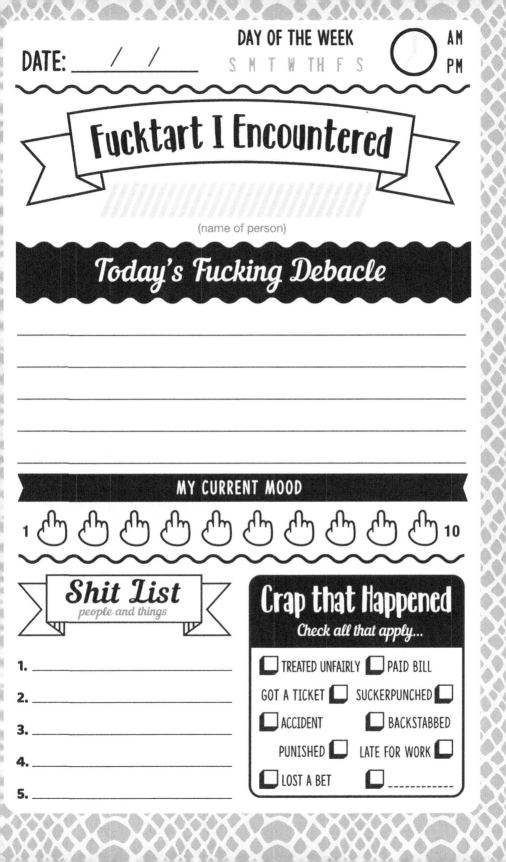

1 ... 10

Shit List
people and things

1. _____

2. _____

3. _____

4. _____

5. _____

Crap that Happened
Check all that apply...

☐ TREATED UNFAIRLY ☐ PAID BILL

GOT A TICKET ☐ SUCKERPUNCHED ☐

☐ ACCIDENT ☐ BACKSTABBED

PUNISHED ☐ LATE FOR WORK ☐

☐ LOST A BET ☐ _____

Bright Spots... It wasn't all bad, was it?

_____
_____
_____
_____
_____
_____
_____
_____
_____

Shit to Do

I'm fortunate to have:

- [ ] _____
- [ ] _____
- [ ] _____
- [ ] _____
- [ ] _____
- [ ] _____

Get your mind off shit &
unscramble profanity:

BDAASRT

answer: bastard

DATE: ___ / ___ / ___

DAY OF THE WEEK

S M T W TH F S

AM
PM

Buttplug I crossed paths with...

(name of person)

Today's [ ] Fiasco

_____
_____
_____
_____
_____

MY CURRENT MOOD

1 👆 👆 👆 👆 👆 👆 👆 👆 👆 👆 10

Shit List
people and things

1. _____

2. _____

3. _____

4. _____

5. _____

"

"

VERBAL DIARRHEA of the DAY

Bright Spots... It wasn't all bad, was it?

_____
_____
_____
_____
_____
_____
_____
_____
_____

"Drink this fuckinated beverage and wake your ass up!"

I'm fortunate to have:

Get your mind off shit w/ some this and that: _Past or future? Save or spend? Asking or answering? Text message or call? Dress shoes or athletic shoes? Smoothies or milkshakes? Paper or plastic? Tiger or elephants? Pierced or clip-on? Lazy or active? City or farm?_

DATE: ___/___/___

DAY OF THE WEEK
S M T W TH F S

AM
PM

Asswipe of the Moment

(name of person)

Today's Crappy Moment

_____

_____

_____

_____

_____

MY CURRENT MOOD

1 👆 👆 👆 👆 👆 👆 👆 👆 👆 👆 10

Shit List
people and things

1. _____

2. _____

3. _____

4. _____

5. _____

Phrase of the Day
Check one...

☐ WHAT THE FUCK   ☐ YOU SUCK ASS

FUCK OFF ☐   WTF R U DOING? ☐

☐ WHO GIVES A SHIT   ☐ EAT SHIT

NICE TRY, DICK ☐   GET THE FUCK OUT ☐

☐ _____

Bright Spots... It wasn't all bad, was it?

_____

_____

_____

_____

_____

_____

_____

_____

Shit to Do

I'm fortunate to have:

☐ _____

☐ _____

☐ _____

☐ _____

☐ _____

☐ _____

Get your mind off shit &
unscramble profanity:

CUUNFKT

DATE: ___ / ___ / ___

DAY OF THE WEEK

S M T W TH F S

AM
PM

Shitbag of the Day

(name of person)

Today's Clusterfuck

_____
_____
_____
_____
_____

MY CURRENT MOOD

1 🖕 🖕 🖕 🖕 🖕 🖕 🖕 🖕 🖕 🖕 10

Shit List
people and things

1. _____
2. _____
3. _____
4. _____
5. _____

Word of the Day
Check all that apply...

☐ SHITTY   ☐ DOUCHEBAG
BRAINFART ☐   BITCHNUGGET ☐
☐ DAMNIT   ☐ FUCKED
ASSHOLE ☐   SHITSTORM ☐
☐ CLUSTERFUCK   ☐ _____

Bright Spots... It wasn't all bad, was it?

_____
_____
_____
_____
_____
_____
_____
_____

"Unfortunately, your idiocy doesn't have an expiration date so I can just throw you out.

I'm fortunate to have:

Get your mind off shit w/ some this and that: Soup or sandwich? Frozen pizza or delivered pizza? Card games or board games? Independent or team player? Wash dishes or mowing lawn? Real plants or fake plants? Outgoing or shy? Project or exams? Movie or play?

DATE: _____ / ___ / _____

DAY OF THE WEEK

S M T W TH F S

AM

PM

Motherfucker of the Hour

(name of person)

Today's Shitty Situation

_____

_____

_____

_____

MY CURRENT MOOD

1 🖕 🖕 🖕 🖕 🖕 🖕 🖕 🖕 🖕 🖕 10

Shit List
people and things

1. _____

2. _____

3. _____

4. _____

5. _____

>>>>>BRAIN FART OF THE DAY<<<<<

Bright Spots... It wasn't all bad, was it?

_____
_____
_____
_____
_____
_____
_____
_____
_____
_____

Shit to Do

I'm fortunate to have:

- ☐ _____
- ☐ _____
- ☐ _____
- ☐ _____
- ☐ _____
- ☐ _____

_Get your mind off shit &
unscramble profanity:_

SBRITHINA

answer: shitbrain

DATE: ___/___/___

DAY OF THE WEEK

S M T W TH F S

AM
PM

Douche Rocket of the Week

(name of person)

Today's Fucking Debacle

_____
_____
_____
_____
_____

MY CURRENT MOOD

1 👆 👆 👆 👆 👆 👆 👆 👆 👆 👆 10

Shit List
people and things

1. _____
2. _____
3. _____
4. _____
5. _____

Crap that Happened
Check all that apply...

☐ TREATED UNFAIRLY ☐ PAID BILL

GOT A TICKET ☐ SUCKERPUNCHED ☐

☐ ACCIDENT ☐ BACKSTABBED

PUNISHED ☐ LATE FOR WORK ☐

☐ LOST A BET ☐ _____

_____

_____

_____

_____

_____

_____

_____

_____

" Kiss my ass but only after I fart in your direction. "

I'm fortunate to have:

Get your mind off shit w/ some this and that: _Long sleeve or short sleeve? Swimming or sun bathing? Black or red? Frozen yogurt or ice cream? Chair or table? Golf or putt-putt? Typing or texting? Party or couch? Classical or Techno? Shoulder bag or clutch?_

DATE: _____ / ___ / _____

DAY OF THE WEEK

S M T W TH F S

AM

PM

Today's Shitstain

(name of person)

Today's ☐ Fiasco

_____

_____

_____

_____

_____

MY CURRENT MOOD

1 🖕 🖕 🖕 🖕 🖕 🖕 🖕 🖕 🖕 🖕 10

Shit List
people and things

1. _____

2. _____

3. _____

4. _____

5. _____

"

"

VERBAL DIARRHEA of the DAY

Bright Spots... It wasn't all bad, was it?

_____
_____
_____
_____
_____
_____
_____
_____
_____

Shit to Do

I'm fortunate to have:

- ☐ _____
- ☐ _____
- ☐ _____
- ☐ _____
- ☐ _____
- ☐ _____

Get your mind off shit & unscramble profanity:

STHAIFEC

DATE: _____ / _____ / _____

DAY OF THE WEEK

S M T W TH F S

AM
PM

Asshat of the Day

(name of person)

Today's Crappy Moment

_____

_____

_____

_____

_____

MY CURRENT MOOD

1 🖕 🖕 🖕 🖕 🖕 🖕 🖕 🖕 🖕 🖕 10

Shit List
people and things

1. _____

2. _____

3. _____

4. _____

5. _____

Phrase of the Day
Check one...

☐ WHAT THE FUCK ☐ YOU SUCK ASS

FUCK OFF ☐ WTF R U DOING? ☐

☐ WHO GIVES A SHIT ☐ EAT SHIT

NICE TRY, DICK ☐ GET THE FUCK OUT ☐

☐ _____

Bright Spots... It wasn't all bad, was it?

_____

_____

_____

_____

_____

_____

_____

> ## "Kill them with kindness. If that fails, tell them to fuck off."

I'm fortunate to have:

Get your mind off shit w/ some this and that: *Bunny or squirrel? Heart or soul? Cake or pie? Chips or popcorn? Hard or soft shell tacos? Hungry or thirsty? Fake or real tree? Sunrise or sunset? Heater or fan? Carpet or hardwood floors? Chicken or beef? Pink or red?*

DATE: ___/___/___

DAY OF THE WEEK

S M T W TH F S

AM
PM

Twatsy of the Hour

(name of person)

Today's Clusterfuck

_____

_____

_____

_____

_____

MY CURRENT MOOD

1 ... 10

Shit List
people and things

1. _____

2. _____

3. _____

4. _____

5. _____

Word of the Day
Check all that apply...

☐ SHITTY   ☐ DOUCHEBAG

BRAINFART ☐   BITCHNUGGET ☐

☐ DAMNIT   ☐ FUCKED

ASSHOLE ☐   SHITSTORM ☐

☐ CLUSTERFUCK   ☐ _____

Bright Spots... It wasn't all bad, was it?

_____
_____
_____
_____
_____
_____
_____
_____
_____

Shit to Do

I'm fortunate to have:

- ☐ _____
- ☐ _____
- ☐ _____
- ☐ _____
- ☐ _____
- ☐ _____

Get your mind off shit & unscramble profanity:

WTTA

answer: twat

DATE: ___ / ___ / ___

DAY OF THE WEEK

S M T W TH F S

AM

PM

Shitass of the Moment

(name of person)

Today's Shitty Situation

_____

_____

_____

_____

_____

MY CURRENT MOOD

1  10

Shit List
people and things

1. _____

2. _____

3. _____

4. _____

5. _____

>>>>>BRAIN FART OF THE DAY<<<<<

_____

_____

_____

_____

_____

_____

_____

_____

"Keep it classy. Hide the fuckery."

I'm fortunate to have:

Get your mind off shit w/ some this and that: Bacon or sausage? Guitar or piano? Hats or headbands? Roses or daisies? Spender or saver? Watch or play sports? Zoo or aquarium? Snakes or badgers? Headphones or earbuds? Tie or no tie? Indie music or classic rock?

DATE: _____ / _____ / _____

DAY OF THE WEEK

S M T W TH F S

AM
PM

Fuckface of the Month

(name of person)

Today's Fucking Debacle

_____

_____

_____

_____

_____

MY CURRENT MOOD

1  10

Shit List
people and things

1. _____

2. _____

3. _____

4. _____

5. _____

Crap that Happened
Check all that apply...

☐ TREATED UNFAIRLY ☐ PAID BILL

GOT A TICKET ☐ SUCKERPUNCHED ☐

☐ ACCIDENT BACKSTABBED ☐

PUNISHED ☐ LATE FOR WORK ☐

☐ LOST A BET ☐ _____

Bright Spots... It wasn't all bad, was it?

_____
_____
_____
_____
_____
_____
_____
_____

Shit to Do

I'm fortunate to have:

- ☐ _____
- ☐ _____
- ☐ _____
- ☐ _____
- ☐ _____
- ☐ _____

Get your mind off shit & unscramble profanity:

UFKCRTAT

answer: fucktart

DATE: ___ / ___ / ___

First Wankjob I thought of today...

(name of person)

Today's [   ] Fiasco

_____

_____

_____

_____

_____

MY CURRENT MOOD

1 🖕 🖕 🖕 🖕 🖕 🖕 🖕 🖕 🖕 🖕 10

Shit List
people and things

1. _____

2. _____

3. _____

4. _____

5. _____

"

"

VERBAL DIARRHEA OF THE DAY

_____

_____

_____

_____

_____

_____

_____

_____

"You better hide because karma's playing hide and seek with you and it's a bitch!"

I'm fortunate to have:

Get your mind off shit w/ some this and that: Shower or tub? Passive or aggressive? Trash or treasure? City or suburbs? Scrambled or sunny side up eggs? Mansion or cabin? Money or fame? Wealth or beauty? Purple or green? Beef jerky or pepperoni stick?

DATE: ___ / ___ / ___

DAY OF THE WEEK

S M T W TH F S

AM
PM

Dick of the Moment

(name of person)

Today's Crappy Moment

_____

_____

_____

_____

_____

MY CURRENT MOOD

1 🖕 🖕 🖕 🖕 🖕 🖕 🖕 🖕 🖕 🖕 10

Shit List
people and things

1. _____

2. _____

3. _____

4. _____

5. _____

Phrase of the Day
Check one...

☐ WHAT THE FUCK   ☐ YOU SUCK ASS

FUCK OFF ☐   WTF R U DOING? ☐

☐ WHO GIVES A SHIT   ☐ EAT SHIT

NICE TRY, DICK ☐   GET THE FUCK OUT ☐

☐ _____

Bright Spots... It wasn't all bad, was it?

_____

_____

_____

_____

_____

_____

_____

_____

Shit to Do

I'm fortunate to have:

- ☐ _____
- ☐ _____
- ☐ _____
- ☐ _____
- ☐ _____
- ☐ _____

Get your mind off shit & unscramble profanity:

SAKJSAC

answer: jackass

DATE: ___ / ___ / ___

DAY OF THE WEEK
S M T W TH F S

AM
PM

Bitch of the Day

(name of person)

Today's Clusterfuck

_____
_____
_____
_____
_____

MY CURRENT MOOD

1 ☝ ☝ ☝ ☝ ☝ ☝ ☝ ☝ ☝ ☝ 10

Shit List
people and things

1. _____
2. _____
3. _____
4. _____
5. _____

Word of the Day
Check all that apply...

☐ SHITTY   ☐ DOUCHEBAG
BRAINFART ☐   BITCHNUGGET ☐
☐ DAMNIT   ☐ FUCKED
ASSHOLE ☐   SHITSTORM ☐
☐ CLUSTERFUCK ☐ _____

_____

_____

_____

_____

_____

_____

_____

_____

_____

"Give me another 10 years, I'm still working on your Bullshit."

I'm fortunate to have:

Get your mind off shit w/ some this and that: Smart or beautiful? Ninjas or robots? Swimming or hiking? Drive or walk? Rock or country? Crushed ice or cubed ice? Water or sparkling water? Candy or cake? Sweet or salty? Singing or dancing? Sunblock or sunscreen?

DATE: ____/____/____

Today's Rimjob

(name of person)

Today's Shitty Situation

_____

_____

_____

_____

_____

MY CURRENT MOOD

1 👆 👆 👆 👆 👆 👆 👆 👆 👆 👆 10

Shit List
people and things

1. _____

2. _____

3. _____

4. _____

5. _____

>>>>>BRAIN FART OF THE DAY<<<<<

Bright Spots... It wasn't all bad, was it?

_____
_____
_____
_____
_____
_____
_____
_____
_____
_____

Shit to Do

- ☐ _____
- ☐ _____
- ☐ _____
- ☐ _____
- ☐ _____
- ☐ _____

I'm fortunate to have:

Get your mind off shit & unscramble profanity:

KERAWN

answer: wanker.

DATE: ___ / ___ / ___

DAY OF THE WEEK

S M T W TH F S

AM
PM

Asshole of the Day

(name of person)

Today's Fucking Debacle

_____

_____

_____

_____

_____

MY CURRENT MOOD

1 👆 👆 👆 👆 👆 👆 👆 👆 👆 👆 10

Shit List
people and things

1. _____

2. _____

3. _____

4. _____

5. _____

Crap that Happened
Check all that apply...

☐ TREATED UNFAIRLY ☐ PAID BILL

GOT A TICKET ☐ SUCKERPUNCHED ☐

☐ ACCIDENT BACKSTABBED ☐

PUNISHED ☐ LATE FOR WORK ☐

☐ LOST A BET ☐ _____

> ## "Shit could be a lot worse. It could be bullshit, instead."

I'm fortunate to have:

Get your mind off shit w/ some this and that: Work or play? Hot weather or cold weather? Sitting or standing? Circles or squares? Invisible or invincible? Spaghetti or alfredo? Painting or drawing? Drive or fly? Chat or gossip? Sweater or hoodies? Art or science?

DATE: _____ / / _____

_____ of the Week

(name of person)

Today's [ ] Fiasco

_____
_____
_____
_____
_____

MY CURRENT MOOD

1 🖕 🖕 🖕 🖕 🖕 🖕 🖕 🖕 🖕 🖕 10

Shit List
people and things

1. _____
2. _____
3. _____
4. _____
5. _____

"

"

VERBAL DIARRHEA of the DAY

Bright Spots... It wasn't all bad, was it?

_____
_____
_____
_____
_____
_____
_____
_____
_____
_____

Shit to Do

I'm fortunate to have:

- ☐ _____
- ☐ _____
- ☐ _____
- ☐ _____
- ☐ _____
- ☐ _____

Get your mind off shit & unscramble profanity:

EMTKRFOEHRCU

answer: motherfucker

DATE: ___ / ___ / ___

DAY OF THE WEEK
S M T W TH F S

AM
PM

Idiot of the Moment

(name of person)

Today's Crappy Moment

_____

_____

_____

_____

_____

MY CURRENT MOOD

1 ☝ ☝ ☝ ☝ ☝ ☝ ☝ ☝ ☝ ☝ 10

Shit List
people and things

1. _____

2. _____

3. _____

4. _____

5. _____

Phrase of the Day
Check one...

☐ WHAT THE FUCK   ☐ YOU SUCK ASS

FUCK OFF ☐   WTF R U DOING? ☐

☐ WHO GIVES A SHIT   ☐ EAT SHIT

NICE TRY, DICK ☐   GET THE FUCK OUT ☐

☐ _____

Bright Spots... It wasn't all bad, was it?

_____

_____

_____

_____

_____

_____

_____

_____

" I'm one glass away from not giving a flying shit. "

I'm fortunate to have:

Get your mind off shit w/ some this and that: _Jalapeno or chili pepper? House party or pool party? Santa or Easter bunny? Neutral tones or bold colors? Sweating or shivering? Burgers or pizza? Flannel or floral? Soda or juice? Stop time or teleportation? Socks or barefoot?_

DATE: ____ / ____ / ____

DAY OF THE WEEK

S M T W TH F S

AM

PM

Fuckface of the Week

(name of person)

Today's Clusterfuck

_____

_____

_____

_____

_____

MY CURRENT MOOD

1  10

Shit List
people and things

1. _____

2. _____

3. _____

4. _____

5. _____

Word of the Day
Check all that apply...

☐ SHITTY   ☐ DOUCHEBAG

BRAINFART ☐   BITCHNUGGET ☐

☐ DAMNIT   ☐ FUCKED

ASSHOLE ☐   SHITSTORM ☐

☐ CLUSTERFUCK   ☐ _____

Bright Spots... It wasn't all bad, was it?

_____
_____
_____
_____
_____
_____
_____
_____
_____
_____

Shit to Do

I'm fortunate to have:

- ☐ _____
- ☐ _____
- ☐ _____
- ☐ _____
- ☐ _____
- ☐ _____

Get your mind off shit &
unscramble profanity:

UTURTTGLSE

answer: gutterslut

AVAILABLE

ON AMAZON.COM

Made in the USA
Coppell, TX
02 November 2022